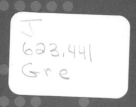

21st Century Skills INNOVATION Library

From Woodpeckers to ... Helmets

by Josh Gregory

INNOVATIONS FROM NATURE

Published in the United States of America by Cherry Lake Publishing
Ann Arbor, Michigan
www.cherrylakepublishing.com

Content Adviser: Robert Friedel, PhD, Professor, Department of History, University of Maryland,
College Park, Maryland

Design: The Design Lab

Photo Credits: Cover and page 3, ©iStockphoto.com/myhrcat; cover (inset), ©FotoVeto/
Shutterstock, Inc.; page 4, ©goldenangel/Shutterstock, Inc.; page 7, ©Jarp2/Shutterstock, Inc.;
page 9, ©Jakez/Shutterstock, Inc.; page 10, ©koi88/Shutterstock, Inc.; page 13, ©JaySi/
Shutterstock, Inc.; page 16, ©Dmitriy Shironosov/Shutterstock, Inc.; page 17, ©Pete Saloutos/
Shutterstock, Inc.; page 19, ©sainthorant daniel/Shutterstock, Inc.; page 20, ©FloridaStock/
Shutterstock, Inc.; page 21, ©Steve Byland/Shutterstock, Inc.; page 23, ©FotoVeto/Shutterstock,
Inc.; page 25, ©Pictorial Press Ltd/Alamy; page 26, ©Everett Collection Inc/Alamy; page 27,
©Ted Pink/Alamy; page 29, ©Brocreative/Shutterstock, Inc.

Library of Congress Cataloging-in-Publication Data
Gregory, Josh.
  From woodpeckers to helmets / by Josh Gregory.
     p. cm.–(Nature's inventors)
  Includes bibliographical references and index.
  ISBN 978-1-61080-495-0 (lib. bdg.) – ISBN 978-1-61080-582-7 (e-book) –
  ISBN 978-1-61080-669-5 (pbk.)
  1. Helmets–Design and construction–Juvenile literature. 2. Woodpeckers–Anatomy–Juvenile
literature. 3. Bones–Juvenile literature. I. Title.
  TP1185.H4G74 2012
  623.4'41–dc23   2012001764

*Cherry Lake Publishing would like to acknowledge
the work of The Partnership for 21st Century Skills.*
Please visit www.21stcenturyskills.org for more information.

*Printed in the United States of America
Corporate Graphics Inc.
July 2012
CLFA11*

CONTENTS

INNOVATIONS FROM   NATURE

CHAPTER ONE

Staying Safe

If you ride a skateboard, you've probably worn a helmet before.

Do you ride a bicycle or skateboard with your friends? Maybe you've played on a football team or an ice hockey team. Wearing a helmet helps make all of these activities much safer. Even if you've never done any of these things, you've probably worn a helmet at some time in your life. People of all ages wear helmets to protect their heads, necks, and faces while doing dangerous things, from playing sports or driving fast vehicles to fighting in wars or working at construction sites.

Your head is one of the most important parts of your body. It is where your brain is located. Your brain controls your body temperature and breathing. It analyzes and acts on information coming from our senses, as well as handling many other tasks. Head injuries can cause serious problems or even result in death. Yet your head is one of the most **fragile** parts of your body. If you're playing baseball and the pitcher throws a fastball that hits you in the leg, you'll probably end up with just a large bruise. But if that same pitch were to hit you in the head, you could very well get a **concussion**.

A concussion is a brain injury caused by a sudden impact to the head. The force of the impact slams the brain against the inside of the skull. Severe concussions can cause **seizures**, memory loss, vomiting, and unconsciousness. Even minor concussions can affect reflexes, speech abilities, and balance. Concussions can also have lasting effects, resulting in serious brain damage. People who suffer numerous concussions, such as some football or hockey players, often experience problems even years after being injured.

Our ears, nose, teeth, and eyes are very fragile, too. They can also be very difficult to repair if they are injured. Severely damaged eyes cannot be replaced. Broken noses do not always look the same once they heal. Facial injuries can leave behind scars that are difficult to hide.

Life & Career Skills

In some places, wearing a helmet is more than just a good idea. It is the law. In the late 1960s, most states began requiring motorcycle drivers to wear helmets. Over the years, these laws have often changed. Today, almost every state has some sort of motorcycle helmet law. Some states require all riders to wear helmets. Others only require riders under 17 years old to wear them. Some states and cities also have laws about wearing bicycle helmets. Whether there is a law in your area or not, wearing a helmet is always a good idea.

To reduce the dangers of head and face injuries, many people wear helmets when playing or working. Different activities bring different risks, so helmets are made in a wide variety of shapes and with different types of materials. For example, motorcycle helmets usually have visors and full face masks to keep sunlight and wind from affecting the driver's vision. They are heavily padded on the inside and very hard on the outside to protect the head from injury. Wrestlers wear a different type of helmet. These are usually made of padded foam and do not cover the entire head. They are not designed to protect against impacts with hard surfaces. Instead, they mainly help prevent ear injuries caused by rubbing against wrestling mats.

Helmets can be designed to do more than protect against impacts. Deep-sea divers wear helmets that provide the air they need to breathe while underwater. These helmets also help divers see clearly and usually

Motorcyclists risk serious injury if they ride without helmets.

contain communication equipment that allows them to speak with people back on the boat. An astronaut's helmet provides many of the same features. A firefighter's helmet is built to withstand incredibly high temperatures without melting.

Like all other technologies, the design of modern helmets is constantly being reviewed, evaluated, and improved. A helmet is an essential piece of safety equipment for all the reasons already given. But designers are still interested in making it that much better. To accomplish this, some have turned their attention to the wild world of animals. Specifically, they have begun to focus on a fascinating bird known as a woodpecker. Woodpeckers get their name from their habit of pecking into solid wood for hours on end. Imagine how painful and damaging this would be for a human being. A woodpecker, however, isn't harmed at all.

Scientists have decided to investigate woodpeckers in the hope of learning their secrets and then using that information to provide the best protection possible. This process of copying nature to create or improve upon existing technologies is known as **biomimicry**. It is one of the fastest-evolving sciences in the world today.

CHAPTER TWO

Helmets Throughout History

Many early helmets protected only the top of the head.

Historians believe that people first began using helmets around 2500 BCE in Sumer, in what is now southern Iraq. These early helmets were probably not inspired by woodpeckers, but rather a simple attempt to provide protection for people's heads. They were constructed from sheets of copper that were shaped to fit over an inner layer of leather or wool. Since then, helmets have been a common part of military equipment around the world. Ancient helmets were made from materials such as iron, bronze, and brass. Many were also made of leather or thick cloth.

As time passed, numerous cultures made important **innovations** in helmet technology. The Assyrians, who lived in what is now northern Iraq and southeastern Turkey, were among the first to give their helmets a high, curved top that came almost to a point. The ancient Greeks and Romans added cheek guards and face guards to their helmets. Around the 13th century, Europeans began using iron **helms**. Medieval knights wore this

Ancient helmets often featured interesting shapes and designs.

type of helmet in battle or during jousting tournaments. Over the years, helmet makers added pieces to helms that provided extra protection for the wearer's neck and face.

Firearms first appeared in Europe in the late 13th century. As these weapons became more powerful and accurate, helmets and other pieces of armor became less effective. By the 1600s, few members of the military wore any armor at all. Things changed during World War I (1914–1918), when soldiers started wearing steel helmets to protect their heads from **shrapnel**. Since then, helmets have been essential pieces of equipment to soldiers everywhere. Advanced scientific breakthroughs have resulted in new high-tech helmets, including ones that are bulletproof, help a soldier see at night, and even help a pilot aim his weapons.

Inventors have often used the basic ideas about military helmets to create protective headwear for other activities. Today, it is common to see people wearing bicycle helmets as they pedal down the street alongside busy traffic. Cyclists first began wearing protective headgear in the 1880s. Some bike riders wore **pith** helmets, which looked more like hats than helmets. They were made of a corklike material and covered in cloth. They were easily crushed and did not provide much protection. In the early 1900s, professional bicycle racers began wearing helmets made of leather straps. These

Learning & Innovation Skills

Learning about ancient history can be tricky and complicated. Researchers must carefully study evidence to find out what life was like thousands of years ago. Sometimes they discover documents written by ancient people. Historians also examine artifacts, which might include drawings or paintings of people wearing helmets, or even actual helmets themselves. Studying these items helps historians learn how ancient helmets were made and used.

helmets did not cover the whole head and provided little protection against crashes. Their main use was to keep cyclists' ears from skidding along the surface of a road during a crash.

The first modern bicycle helmets were invented in the 1970s. **Engineers** working on new technology for motorcycle helmets used their ideas to create a new kind of bicycle helmet. In 1975, Bell Helmets, Inc., began selling a bicycle helmet that consisted of a thick layer of foam covered by a thin layer of hard plastic. The helmet was lightweight and strong enough to protect against impacts. By the 1980s, bicycle helmets had become popular among all types of cyclists, from professional racers to everyday riders.

Hard hats are another type of helmet often seen today. You can easily spot them being worn around construction sites and other workplaces where falling **debris** is a danger. The first hard hats were invented in the early 20th century. Until that time, miners had

People of all ages use bike helmets to stay safe when they ride.

been wearing leather caps. Shortly after World War I, E. W. Bullard used the steel helmets worn by soldiers as inspiration for a new mining helmet. The first hard hats were made of canvas that was steamed and glued into a hard, durable shape. Later versions were made of aluminum and fiberglass. In the 1950s, Bullard's company began making plastic hard hats like the ones used today. Plastic is cheaper and easy to mold into shapes. It also does not conduct electricity, which provides extra protection to people working where there is danger of being electrocuted.

Sports helmets are another type of protective headgear that is widely used. It's hard to imagine a time when players did not have any head protection at all. Yet in the earliest days of our most popular sports, helmets were not available.

Football players first started strapping on helmets in the late 1890s. Like other early helmets, they were made mainly of leather. They fit over the player's head and covered his ears. A strap was fastened near the Adam's apple using a buckle. Like early bicycle helmets, these helmets did not do much to protect against head impacts but instead protected the player's ears. During the 1920s, the part of the helmet protecting the top of the head was made harder and stronger. The new helmets worked better than earlier models but were still far from perfect.

Finally, in 1939, the first plastic football helmets were made. They were shaped almost exactly like modern helmets, but lacked face masks and were not quite as strong. That same year, players began using chinstraps, which secured the helmet by wrapping around the chin rather than the neck. Chinstraps were much safer and more comfortable. Face masks were introduced the following year. These innovations met with great success during the 1940s, and the National Football League (NFL) soon began requiring all players to wear them.

Baseball players are especially at risk for head injuries when at bat. A pitched ball hitting a batter's head can cause a concussion, crack the skull, or even kill. Yet batting helmets did not become common in baseball until the 1950s. Before then, a few batters experimented with leather helmets similar to those used in other sports. Other players slipped plastic or metal plates into their baseball caps. These efforts helped protect a player's head, but not many players were eager to wear them.

The first plastic baseball helmets were produced in the 1940s. These were lightweight but hard and durable, and could fit over the player's baseball cap. Baseball teams began encouraging their players to wear these new helmets, and they quickly became popular. Finally, in the late 1950s, protective headgear became required for all players, from professionals to Little League players. Earflaps were soon added to Little League helmets to protect batters' ears, and these became required for professional ballplayers in the 1970s.

Today's Helmets

Modern helmets keep their wearers safe without weighing them down.

Modern helmets are much safer and more durable than the helmets from years past. They are built to survive incredible abuse while remaining lightweight enough for wearers to play sports or do their jobs. New kinds of plastic are often lighter and stronger than older forms were. New foams can absorb heavier shocks than previous types. Lighter helmets are more comfortable for the wearer, and people are much

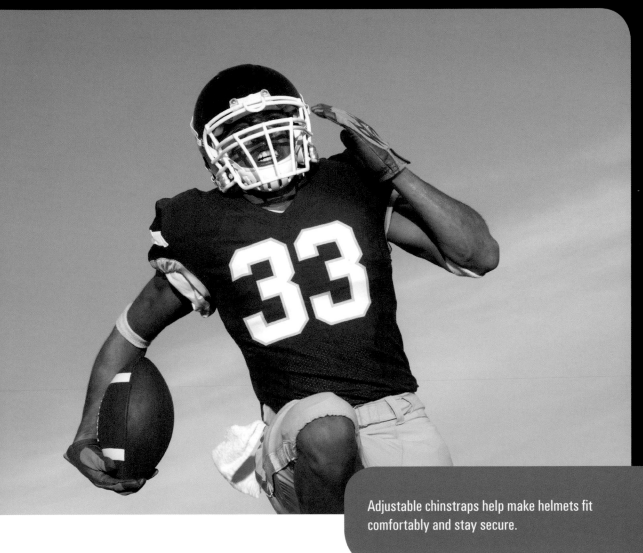

Adjustable chinstraps help make helmets fit comfortably and stay secure.

more likely to wear helmets if they are comfortable. Heavy, bulky helmets can cause neck strain.

Innovations have made helmets easier to put on and take off. Today's helmet straps often use buckles or snaps that can be easily shut or pulled apart at the press of a button. They can also be adjusted to fit different head sizes. Tight helmets can be very uncomfortable, and loose

21st Century Content

Some modern helmets feature a variety of electronic equipment to make them even more useful. Professional and college football quarterbacks often have radios and microphones built into their helmets that allow them to communicate with coaches on the sidelines. Military pilots use similar technology to communicate with one another in flight and back on the ground.

Some football helmets also contain computers that record the details of each impact upon the helmet. The computers measure how powerful each hit is and where it strikes the helmet. Players can use this information to make sure they are using proper form when colliding with other players, and doctors can use it to discover the exact causes of a player's head injuries.

ones cannot always protect against injuries. Helmets must fit perfectly in order to work well.

New helmet shapes have also helped to improve their use. Bicycle helmets are made to be **aerodynamic** so that they do not slow down the rider. Motorcycle and motocross helmets extend out and around the jaw to protect the wearer's face. Many bicycle, skateboard, and motocross helmets have built-in visors to help keep sunlight out of the wearer's eyes. Most helmets have vents that allow air to flow through them, keeping the user's head cool.

Despite using such groundbreaking technology, helmets are still far from perfect. Football players frequently experience concussions due to the force and frequency of receiving blows to the head. Researchers believe repeated concussions cause other problems later in life, including a variety of mental illnesses. This is why it has

Motocross helmets are designed to block sunlight and protect the wearer's face.

become so important to study woodpeckers. Relatively speaking, a human being could not survive the beating a woodpecker's head takes on any given day. However, woodpeckers never suffer any physical or mental damage. Designers are now trying to imagine what could result from copying these birds' natural abilities.

CHAPTER FOUR

New Possibilities

Even though they are often very small birds, woodpeckers can quickly drill huge holes into trees.

Woodpeckers are the natural choice to serve as models for improved helmet design. They have perhaps the greatest natural helmets in the world. These remarkable creatures can quickly make holes in the toughest trees by essentially beating their beaks against the wood until it crumbles apart. Some woodpeckers use the holes to store food for the cold winter months. Others build nests inside.

Some woodpeckers dig holes to make nests for their babies.

Many are simply looking for food such as insects or tree sap. The tiny birds hammer away until they have dug through the surface of the tree, and then use their long tongues to feed. The loud sound of their pecking also serves a purpose, warning off rivals and attracting mates.

Learning & Innovation Skills

When Sang-Hee Yoon and Sungmin Park began their woodpecker research at the University of California, Berkeley, they were not trying to discover new technologies to improve helmets. However, their work could lead to the creation of helmets unlike any ever built. Sometimes experiments result in new discoveries that the researcher never imagined. For example, Play-Doh, the odd-smelling claylike stuff you probably used to mold into shapes when you were younger, was not meant to be a toy. It was originally invented to clean wallpaper!

Woodpeckers slam their beaks into wood at speeds of 13 to 15 miles (21 to 24 kilometers) per hour. They can peck about 18 to 22 times per second. On average, they bang their heads against hard surfaces about 12,000 times every day. Each one of those impacts is about 100 times as powerful as a hit that would cause a concussion in a human. Yet somehow, woodpeckers are not harmed. Why not?

In early 2011, researchers Sang-Hee Yoon and Sungmin Park from the University of California, Berkeley, published a paper detailing how woodpeckers manage to avoid hurting themselves as they pound away at hard surfaces. The researchers learned that woodpeckers have spongy bones in their heads rather than hard, brittle ones. Woodpeckers also have beaks that are hard, yet flexible. Yoon and Park also noticed that there is very little space for a woodpecker's brain to move around inside its skull. They concluded that the flexibility of the various parts of a woodpecker's head helps to absorb vibrations, which softens the blow of impacts.

The researchers decided to build mechanical devices that imitated the functions of a woodpecker's spongy bones and flexible beak. Their goal was to improve black boxes, the devices on airplanes that keep detailed records of a flight. Black boxes are used to analyze what went wrong when an airplane crashes, so they must be able to withstand the impact of falling from the sky.

A woodpecker's head is built to withstand extreme force.

The researchers placed the black box's technology inside a steel container of tightly packed, tiny glass beads. This was done to reproduce the hard, yet spongy texture of a woodpecker's skull. They covered the container with a layer of rubber to absorb vibrations and then covered the whole thing with a layer of aluminum. The project was a great success: the new black box was 60 times more protective than older types.

From the positive and exciting results of the black box project came another realization. If woodpecker-inspired technology worked so well there, it would probably also work well in the improvement of helmet design. Two Chinese scientists, Yubo Fan and Ming Zhang, decided to look into this more closely. In 2011, they published the results of their research. To study the woodpeckers closely, they created computer models of the birds' heads. Using high-speed video cameras, they filmed the woodpeckers so they could watch footage of the pecking in super slow motion. They came to many of the same conclusions as Yoon and Park, but they also noticed the importance of the shape of a woodpecker's beak. The top part of the beak is longer than the bottom half. When it slams into a tree, it bends down and back, absorbing some of the impact. The researchers believe that these discoveries could be very useful in developing new helmets. In fact, the U.S. Army and several helmet manufacturers are already hard at work searching for ways to use the research.

CHAPTER FIVE

Pioneers of Protection

Many scientists and inventors have helped contribute to the improvement of helmet technology throughout the years. Here are just a couple of them:

Franz Kafka (1883–1924) is best known as one of the most important writers of the 20th century. Works such as *The Metamorphosis* and *The Trial* have been read widely for decades.

While Franz Kafka is mainly remembered for his writing, he may also have invented the hard hat.

John T. Riddell's helmet design helped protect
American soldiers during World War II.

Today, Riddell football helmets are worn by all NFL players.

However, some sources also credit him as a pioneer in helmet design. As a young man, Kafka worked at an insurance company. Part of his job involved learning about the injuries suffered by people working dangerous jobs. Sometime between 1910 and 1912, he is believed to have invented the hard hat, a lightweight helmet designed to protect against falling objects in factories. Hard hats continue to protect the heads of workers at construction sites, factories, and other dangerous work environments today.

John T. Riddell (1885–1945) was the inventor of several important kinds of sports equipment that are still used widely today. In 1922, he invented removable football cleats, which allowed players to better grip the surface of the ground as they ran. In 1939, he created his most well-known invention, the plastic football helmet. It worked so well that the U.S. military used some of Riddell's ideas to create the helmets its troops wore during World War II (1939–1945). Today, Riddell's company continues to manufacture the NFL's official helmets.

Today's helmets have come a long way since their earliest versions.

Glossary

aerodynamic (air-oh-dye-NAM-mik) designed to move through the air very quickly and easily

artifacts (ART-uh-fakts) objects made or changed by human beings, especially tools or weapons used in the past

biomimicry (bye-oh-MI-mi-kree) the practice of copying nature in order to build or improve something

concussion (kuhn-KUSH-uhn) an injury to the brain caused by a heavy blow to the head

debris (duh-BREE) the scattered pieces of something that has been broken or destroyed

engineers (en-juh-NIHRZ) people who are trained to design and build machines, vehicles, or other structures

fragile (FRAJ-il) delicate or easily broken

helms (HELMZ) headpieces of ancient or medieval armor

innovations (in-uh-VAY-shuhnz) new ideas or inventions

patents (PAT-uhnts) legal documents giving the inventor of an item sole rights to manufacture or sell the item

pith (PITH) a soft, spongy tissue found in certain plants and used to make early helmets

seizures (SEE-zhurz) sudden attacks of illness or spasms

shrapnel (SHRAP-nel) small pieces of metal thrown out by an exploding shell or bomb

For More Information

BOOKS

Blaxland, Wendy. *Helmets*. New York: Marshall Cavendish Benchmark, 2011.

Murray, Julie. *Woodpeckers*. Edina, MN: ABDO Publishing Company, 2005.

WEB SITES

Daily *Mail Online*—"Protective Nature: How Woodpeckers Could Help Improve Helmet Technology to Prevent Brain Injuries"
www.dailymail.co.uk/news/article-2054007/Woodpecker-answer-creating-better-helmets-preventing-brain-injuries.html
Read this article describing the findings of woodpecker researchers and look at a diagram of a woodpecker's head.

Riddell—History
www.riddell.com/innovation/history/
Look at a timeline showing the evolution of football helmets from thin, leather hats to the strong, plastic models used today.

Index

About the Author

Josh Gregory writes and edits books for kids. He lives in Chicago, Illinois.